THE BEST OF YOU

Inspirational Pearls of Wisdom

OHENEYERE GIFTY ANTI

THE BEST OF YOU

Inspirational Pearls of Wisdom

OHENEYERE GIFTY ANTI

The Best of You
© 2020 Oheneyere Gifty Anti

To contact the author,
call GDA Media Ltd. on 0543 618 182.

Worldwide Distribution: Triple A Press

Designed by
BUABENG BOOKS
Email: info@buabengcommunications.com
Website: www.buabengcommunications.com/
BuabengBooks

Acknowledgement

To my staff:

Pearl Amoah Amponsah, Daniel Sugmen Atule, Mumin Mohammed-Deifullah, Jeremiah Abbey, Andrews Ohene Ampofo, Emmanuel Ashley, who worked hard to get GDA Media Ltd and The Standpoint running while I concentrated on writing, I say thank you. I appreciate you all.

To Lydia Agyapomaa who sacrificed her time and business to help take care of my daughter whenever I had to travel or busy with work, God bless you and may that miracle happen this year.

To the volunteers who are always ready to help us with work, recordings, charities and programmes, I am grateful.

And to Kobbi Blaq for his support and Kennedy Bentum Jnr of KennyVille Experience for taking the cover photo. To Naa Korkoi Quaye of Naak's Beauty Studio. You are blessed.

Indeed, you can only excel, when you have the right support systems.

Dedication

This book is dedicated to my little girl, Nyame Animuonyam Afia Asaa Afrakoma Sintim- Misa.

May you grow and achieve greater things that I can only dream of. May you never make the mistakes I have made in my life.

May your life's journey bring glory to God, your parents, family, nation, continent and the world.

My sunshine, thank you for choosing me as your mother. Thank you for making me experience motherhood.

Introduction

My first book, *A Bit of Me,* became a most sought-after inspirational book for many Ghanaians in and outside Ghana.

It resonated with the life of many that read the book. One of the things that also stood out for them was the phrases and what some referred to as 'quotable quotes'.

The Best of You, therefore, is to help people read and own the short sentences, phrases and quotes that can inspire and motivate them to be the best of themselves.

This is easy to read and imbibe the words. If you like, you can call it Gifty's Daily Inspirational and Motivational Pep Talk.

As beautiful as the picture on the cover of this book may look, the lines under my eyes and my grey hair tell stories; stories of my hassle, my pain, my joy, my struggle, my success.

In short, they tell the story of my journey so far. My dear, WEAR YOUR SCARS BEAUTIFULLY. They are part of your journey, your story. And keep smiling because you are beautiful.

Gifty Anti

My dear friend, please remember, that where you are, what you are going through right now, is not who you are. Life happens, circumstances change. Hard times will come but they will not last forever. The waiting period is painful, but it is a phase, it will soon pass. Hold on. Don't lose who you are. You are beautiful. Keep that smile.

Gifty Anti

Do you know that you can laugh over or be upset about the same thing, depending on your mood? Choose ye this day what it's going to be! Are you going to laugh over the challenges, disappointments, betrayals, failures or foolishness of others towards you? Or are you going to be upset and let it mess up your day? You have a choice.

Gifty Anti

My dear one, it is not everything we crave for, desire, admire, fantasize about, that is good for us or we must have. Some things are just meant to be dreamt about. Some things are just meant to be admired. You must not necessarily have it, do it or be a part of it. It's not every battle you must fight.

Gifty Anti

Choosing to be happy is not an indication that you have it all sorted out. It does not mean you have no problems, no hurts, no challenges. It simply means you know it will get better one day. It means you are grateful for the gift of life. It means you acknowledge your imperfections and learnt lessons from the cards that life has offered. It means you trust God to fix it.

Gifty Anti

There is dignity in hard work. There is pride in earning your keep. You are not too beautiful, too intelligent, too powerful or too something to do 'certain jobs'. Whatever you do, be passionate and diligent about it. Own it and be proud of it. You will be amazed what will come out of it. And never ever, let success 'get into your head'. There is always more you can do and achieve.

Gifty Anti

07

Remember, you cannot control what others do to you or how they treat you.

Well, most of the time you may do your best, but they will still treat you badly, betray you, disappoint or hurt you.

However, you have absolute control over how you treat people or what you do to them. It's your choice.

Who do you choose to be? How do you choose to treat people? What do you choose to do? Think about it.

Gifty Anti

08

Let's stop the societal pressures of defining what, how, who a person must and has to be. Let's allow people to live with their flaws.

Let's allow them to fail, make mistakes without 'shaming them into oblivion'. Mistakes are part of life. Failures are what we need to build on, to become better human beings.

Every now and then ask yourself, I failed and so what? I have made mistakes and so what? I didn't get it right and so what? I didn't succeed... AND SO WHAT?

Let's allow people to live their choices. Live your choices.

Gifty Anti

It's ok not to be ok. Its ok to live your life being happy. It is ok to fail. It is ok to make mistakes. We all have failed before and made mistakes. We will definitely make some more mistakes and fail at something again. But it is ok.

Our forefathers from the day of Adam, failed and made mistakes. Sorry to disappoint you my dear, but, it did not start with you and it won't end with you.

Gifty Anti

11

10

If people are not cutting you a slack, cut yourself some slack and move on from toxic energy. DON'T BE AFRAID. DON'T LET THEIR GOSPEL OF FEAR PREVENT YOU FROM BEING HAPPY. One day, you will look back and laugh. You will make it. You will win your battles. Hold on. Don't give up. It will get better. Remember, SUCCESS COMES IN MANY WAYS. Shalom.

Gifty Anti

Before you go to sleep and when you wake up, I want you to know this; a cheat does not need a reason to cheat. No! A cheat, cheats because he or she is a cheat. Stop blaming yourself. Stop being miserable.

You have cried enough over something that is no fault of yours. Wipe your tears. Rise up and wise up! The danger is not just who he or she cheats with. The danger is the disease and infections 'they' will bring your way.

The danger is the 'brokenness' and 'self-destructive' path their cheating can lead you to.

Rise up and wise up.

Gifty Anti

Do your best in everything because you are the best and leave the rest to God. Be a better person because you deserve to be a better human being. Change, reform, adapt etc. for yourself, not for anyone. And please, never ever give up on yourself.

Gifty Anti

THE ORIGINAL - There is beauty in originality. There is sexiness in originality. You can only be successful if you are and stay original. Learn from others. Take inspiration from others. But please don't ever copy anyone. Don't be the duplicate or photocopy of someone. That person has succeeded because he or she is the original. Stay original.

Gifty Anti

WHEN QUITTERS WIN - I know it is said that quitters don't win and winners don't quit. But sometimes you need to quit to win. Note, I said SOMETIMES .

Gifty Anti

POWER - What a powerful word!!! They say power corrupts and absolute power corrupts absolutely. I totally disagree. I believe power brings out our true nature and character. How we behave when we have power, is the true us. What I seek, is not power. What I desperately seek to achieve in life, is to inspire, motivate and ultimately, impact lives.

And having power (by virtue of the platforms and leverage I have) of course makes it easy to reach and impact lives. Do you want power? What for? What are you doing with the power you already have? May God keep us humble, no matter how powerful we become in life.

Gifty Anti

16

Dear one, always remember, that NO ONE WAS BORN FOOLISH. People choose to BE FOOLISH. May we choose to BE WISE, KIND, COMPASSIONATE, LOVING AND

FOCUSED. *Gifty Anti*

17

There comes a time, when you scream so loud, yet no one seems to hear your screams. Not even the ones closest to you seem to hear your screams.

You just don't understand why no one seems to notice or understand your screams. But the truth is, your screams are deep inside. It is not audible. You are unable to let it out.

Despite the beautiful smiles, you are dying inside, hoping someone would hear and show you some love. God hears your screams and He will fill your mouth with laughter today. It shall be well. It is well. Today, you will laugh again.

Gifty Anti

Most of the time, those who try to drag you into the gutter with them, have nothing to lose. But you do. Your dignity, pride, image etc. You have a lot to lose. So watch it! Don't let them drag you there with them. You don't belong in the gutter with them. Watch it!

Gifty Anti

It is more difficult to IGNORE than to respond to the foolish. But the wise and strong-willed IGNORES, knowing that you cannot make a foolish person understand WISDOM. When you pray, pray for wisdom and strength to ignore the Foolish. Selah!!!

Gifty Anti

20

"Sometimes bitterness, hurt, hatred can give you a false sense of power! But remember, the catch word is FALSE. Real power is being in absolute control of your emotions. Take charge of your emotions. Know your source of real power".

Gifty Anti

Decency is not just about how you dress or how you look. Decency is also about how you speak, what you say, the words you use and how you use them. Your attitude, character and behaviour also matter greatly when it comes to decency.

Gifty Anti

Sometimes, you may not feel right about something but you still have to try it. It may or may not work for you. But you may never know until you try it. It's called RISK. Don't be afraid to take risks. But take sensible, well calculated and 'thought-through' RISKS, leaving your options open.

Gifty Anti

23

I don't do 'everybody or somebody'. I do Me. 'Me' is the most powerful asset I have. And it will take God and Me to succeed in life!! Find your 'Me' and use it.

Gifty Anti

'My situation, position or title, does not make me great. I make my situation, position or title great. I am the 'greatness' that happens and change the position, situation or title. My Greatness is defined by God'. You are great, so pursue greatness.

Gifty Anti

When God moves you to the next level, don't go fighting battles from your previous level. Know, accept and operate in your new level.

Gifty Anti

My dear one, not everyone who criticizes you hates you. Some really mean well. I admit, most of the time, our critics are very harsh. They come across as though they are attacking or condemning us. But if you can react positively by not letting the criticism destroy you, you will always come out a better person.

Gifty Anti

In everything, tone matters. How you talk matters. The tone in every conversation or discourse is important. You cannot live in this world not caring about who you hurt or offend.

Gifty Anti

"Knowing your enemies, especially those close to you, who pretend to be with you, is a blessing. May God reveal and take away those in life to steal, destroy or to kill from us". May we know them and be wary of them. But live not in fear. God has got you. Just pray.

Gifty Anti

Never ever let disagreement on an issue come between you and a good relationship. It is not right. It doesn't show maturity. It is not intelligent. It is not wise. It is not cool. It is not sexy. It is not bae. It is not Godly. Learn to love and live beyond disagreements, no matter how passionate you are about the issue.

Gifty Anti

"I am not pushed to inspire for fame. I only inspire when I am inspired to inspire. Never do anything for the sake of fame. Do it because you believe in it. Following God's direction makes the difference. True Inspiration comes from God".

Gifty Anti

"I was achieving as Gifty Anti. I am Achieving as OHENEYERE Gifty Anti. And I will Achieve as Gifty Anti. It's all about what I carry within and not what I acquire. Always seek what no one can take from you".

Gifty Anti

"I married at the age 45, rather late. But there are still things I wish I had done and achieved before then. Enjoy your singleness. It's a blessing not a curse".

Gifty Anti

"There is no limitation to what you can achieve. Your dream may seem ridiculous to someone, but it may be your pathway to greatness. It may be your step to success".

Gifty Anti

34

You will have to make compromises, sacrifices and sometimes change your attitude for the good and benefit of 'the people'.... of society. So yes, by all means be you. Hold on to your beliefs and opinions.

But know that once you hold a position of authority or in the public space you cannot totally ignore what society thinks or expects of you.

If it's not harmful to you, if it doesn't demean you, if it doesn't take away your pride as a human being, then yes, you have to do what society expects of you.

Gifty Anti

I am a strong believer of doing my best and leaving the rest to God. But sometimes, I just get tired of doing my best and don't feel like doing anything. Sometimes, I simply get fed up - tired and fed up. But I know It's okay because I am only but human. It's okay to be fed up sometimes. You see, I have learnt that sometimes. God doesn't need us to do anything. He wants to do it all by Himself.

Gifty Anti

41

36

Sometimes, all you need to keep moving is a kind word from a loved one, family or friends. Sometimes, all you need to keep striving, pushing etc., is a show of gratitude. But sometimes, the very people you are killing yourself for or sacrificing for don't even seem to care. Sometimes, it's as if they don't see your struggles, achievements, kindness etc. Sometimes, it's as if they are taking you for granted and most of the times, they are. Sometimes, that really hurts, so badly you just want to give up.

I just want you to know that God sees it all. He sees all you do; your sacrifices, your pains, your bleeding. He sees it all. So please don't give up, don't stop doing good, don't stop loving, don't stop caring, don't, don't, don't stop.

Gifty Anti

My dear one, it's ok to cry. Crying may not 'solve the problem' but sometimes, actually most of the time, crying makes you feel better! Sometimes, you feel better after a good cry so cry if and when you feel like it. And always remember, crying may last for the night but joy will definitely come 'in the morning'. So, after crying, wipe your tears and move on.

Gifty Anti

Sometimes in doing the right thing, it feels like you have been "sent back' a million steps from where you used to be. You virtually lose everything. Family, loved ones and friends who could help, desert you, your debtors come chasing you, etc. You find yourself struck by the "job syndrome". Hold on for your Testimony is coming. It's part of your journey. Good times are coming.

Gifty Anti

There comes a time when you can't help it; you just miss your past. There were some really good times and things in our past. However, the future can be so much better. Enjoy today and hold on to the future. God is always Faithful.

Gifty Anti

Every now and then your past 'remembers' you and comes smiling at you. Your past was not that bad. Don't be too hard on yourself.

Gifty Anti

41

Let not your past experiences blind you, harden your heart or turn you into a bitter human being. The fact that you have been betrayed before does not mean all human beings are bad.

The fact that you have had a bad marriage, does not mean marriage is bad. The fact that you have been abused before does not mean all men are abusive.

It does not mean all women are wicked. Be careful not to generalize based on your past or present experiences. And do not let other people's bad experiences influence your life. Remember, we may have the same problems, but our solutions may differ.

Gifty Anti

We all have different journeys but our paths may cross sometimes. But it does not mean we are on the same journey or have the same destiny. Your journey is different and so is your story. Good people still exist. Don't lose faith in your journey. Learn from other people's mistakes or their stories but make your own mistakes. Have your own experiences. And through it all, don't forget that God is real and He is Faithful. I wish you well on your journey.

Gifty Anti

Don't worry about what you could have been. It is past. But please, don't lose sight of what you can be or what you can become. So do not dare move from the Super Crazy Faith Street. Your miracle is on its way. Don't move.

Gifty Anti

Dear one, being single at a 'certain age' can be very tough; really tough, no matter how strong you are. Not because you are desperate, but because of what society, family, loved ones etc, will throw at you. But remember, singleness is not a curse. It is a blessing and offers you the opportunity to do and achieve so much before you finally decide or choose to marry or not.

Gifty Anti

45

Have you ever had to sacrifice for someone who doesn't deserve it? Have you ever had to sacrifice for someone whom you knew will not do the same for you? Not easy. Herrrr… It is very painful. Trust me, I know that feeling too well. It is so painful.

And the worse one is, have you ever had to sacrifice for someone who you know, will not show gratitude or appreciation? You feel so stupid and annoyed. But the question is, why do you even make that sacrifice? Do you really have to? What do you lose if you don't do it? And what do you gain if you do it?

Well, I am here to tell you that it's okay to make that sacrifice. You are not a fool. You are not stupid. In the long run, it is very satisfying to know that you did your best for humanity. That is what makes you human. You are not a fool. You are only being human and Godly.

Gifty Anti

There is a 'Dark Side' to everything and everyone. No matter how well intended the concept, idea, programme etc. or person is, there are always those who will 'work it to the dark side'. There are those who will manipulate it to serve a certain dark or negative purpose or agenda. Some call them extremists. Others call them evil. Stay true to what you believe in; your values, your principles. Be sensitive in your spirit always. And keep a clean heart.

Gifty Anti

Be kind to yourself. Love yourself. Treat yourself; your health, your emotions and your heart well. Feed your mind, your soul, body and spirit with good things in life. Surround yourself with good energy and people who truly care and love you, irrespective of their race, age, gender, educational or social background. And smile, laugh a lot, because you are beautiful.

Gifty Anti

48

Life is full of challenges, uncertainties and unforeseen circumstances. But be determined not to let your challenges hold you captive. So please, smile, laugh, give, love and move on.

Gifty Anti

49

One of the difficult things to do in life, is to let go of your bitterness. Bitterness is possessive. Once it gets into your heart, it is difficult, very difficult to evict it.

But you have to let bitterness go. You have to evict it because bitterness is a stinking spirit that drives away every happiness, joy, contentment, fulfilment, gratitude and growth from your heart.

Whatever has brought this bitterness to your heart, please let it go. It is not easy but you can let it go one day at a time.

Try it and you will see how your life will turn around for your good.

Gifty Anti

50

I always tell my colleague married women that every mother in-law is a witch until we also become a mother in-law.

Motherhood is tough and the sacrifices that most mothers make for their children give them a certain sense of entitlement to their children for life.

Treat your mother in-law like your mother but remember she did not give birth to you.

I know some mothers-in-law can be real pain, but try hard not to be the cause of pain or conflict

between a mother and her son. You will win
the battle eventually.

Gifty Anti

51

In my 50 years on earth, I have had some women who have shown me real pepper. Smh! But you know what? I have had some great women who have been my support and angels too.

Ignorance and certain negative human attitudes sometimes push some women to treat other women badly.

But don't get it twisted. It's a human thing not a women thing.

Don't live your life believing women are their own enemies. Every woman needs her tribe of women, her sisterhood. Don't forget it.

Gifty Anti

52

Do not fear the 'woman sitting next to you'. Fear the human being who means you evil, even though he or she smiles with you. Evil has no gender my dear. Human beings are potentially evil. But my dear, live, love and laugh like you have never been hurt. Life happens. It will get better.

Gifty Anti

You can't live without your family; No, you can't live without them. No matter how loud the world hails you, your joy can never be complete if your 'family' is not there to cheer you on. Treasure your family. Love them and do your best for and with them. Money is not always the answer to every problem. The 'human touch' makes a greater impact.

Gifty Anti

54

On 23rd January, 2020, I turned 50-My golden jubilee. I was so excited and to know why I was excited you have to read my Golden book, 50 Nuggets @ 50. That is if you haven't read it yet.

In the midst of my excitement, I was literally forced to pause and reflect and ask myself some questions.

So far, what? Good or bad? What are the next years going to be? Business as usual? Or I am going to up my gain?

My dear, no matter how far you think you have come in life, there is a lot more you can achieve.

Gifty Anti

There are times we go through the 'midnight hour'. The '11th hour' when it seems all is lost. It can be scary you know. Actually, it is always scary. But fear not. My God of the 11th hour is about to deliver you. But, are you ready for your miracle? Are you ready to receive the testimony? God has never failed me and He will never fail you. Hold on to Him!

Gifty Anti

In my 50 years of existence, I have also realized, that no matter how hard you try, no matter the sacrifices you make, there will always be that person or people, who will try to paint you 'black'. People will try to destroy your brand or reputation. But God's will for you, for me, for us will always stand. Like the moon that shines through the night, like the stars that light up the dark clouds, we will always shine. Fear not. God is Faithful.

Gifty Anti

57

Sometimes, you can't help but to wonder, "does God love some people more than others?". Why does God watch while evil people thrive and prosper? I am sure you have had such thoughts many times. God loves all of us and you see the evil person thriving is because you are focusing on the evil one and not focusing on God. Focus on God and keep moving.

Gifty Anti

58

God knows what we need at what time. His timing for us is different. He glorifies Himself in His own time and His timing is always right. He is always on time. It doesn't matter when He shows up. Trust Him. You will be shocked what He is about to do in your life. Don't doubt Him. It will all make sense in the end.

Gifty Anti

There is nothing you cannot achieve, if you put your mind to it and you are determined. But remember, it should be at your own pace. In your own time. Let no one push you or shame you into doing it. Do it for yourself. Go on my dear. Dare to be you.

Gifty Anti

Life is a journey and you have to make a conscious effort to enjoy the journey. Happiness is a priceless asset and a catalyst to success and achievement. Serve yourself Happiness so others can also enjoy it when you serve it.

Gifty Anti

OHENEYERE DR. GIFTY ANTI
(AWO DANSOA of Akwamu Adumasa)

Oheneyere Gifty Anti is a multiple award-winning broadcast journalist with 22 years working experience. She is the C. E. O. of GDA Media, a media production company. She is the host of her own show, the award winning women's discussion programme, The Standpoint since 2008.

She is a motivational and conference speaker and has spoken on many platforms and at educational institutions across Ghana and beyond. She holds a Master's Degree in International Journalism from City University, London. She also holds a Diploma in Journalism from the Ghana Institute of Journalism. She is a proud product of Mfantsiman Girls Secondary

School. Oheneyere, as she is now affectionately called, currently holds an Honorary Doctor of Letters Degree.

She currently has about 37 awards to her name including;

- 100 most powerful speakers 2018 by Speakers Bureau Africa

- Ghana Outstanding Women Awards - 2018

- 18th Most Influential Ghanaian – 2016 (Only Female In First 20)

- Life Time Achievement Award for Excellence in Media- 2018

- Overall Female Young Professional Role Model Of The Year, 2013

- The African Women In Leadership Organisation's, Awlo, Excellence Award For "Giving Women A Platform And A Voice"

2013.

Her love and passion for the Ghanaian culture and tradition has earned her an honour by the Bonwire Kente weavers.

She was also honoured by the Manya Krobo Traditional Council with the title Yokama (a virtuous woman).

Oheneyere Gifty Anti is the President and founder of the Girl in Need Foundation, GiNF and Awo Dansoa Reading Project, ADRP.

She is married to Nana Ansah Kwao IV, Chief of Akwamu Adumasa and they have a daughter, Nyame Animuonyam Afia Asaa Afrakoma Sintim Misa (Ahenkan - The Princess of Adumasa).